So You Want to Be Mentored:

An Application Workbook for Using Five Strategies to Get the Most out of a Mentoring Relationship

Stella Louise Cowan

HRD Press, Inc. • Amherst • Massachusetts

Published by: HRD Press, Inc.
                22 Amherst Road
                Amherst, Massachusetts 01002
                1-800-822-2801 (U.S. and Canada)
                1-413-253-3488
                1-413-253-3490 (fax)
                http://www.hrdpress.com

ISBN: 0-87425-928-2

Production services by Anctil Virtual Office
Cover design by Eileen Klockars
Editorial services by Suzanne Bay

Contents

List of Tools

How to Use
This Workbook

This book can be used in a number of ways. For example, it can serve as:

- A self-study workbook
- A guide for a facilitator-led training workshop
- A source of "à la carte" application tools to help make you a better protégé (surveys, checklists, worksheets, models, etc.)
- A general reference book on mentoring

There are over three dozen helpful application tools. Feel free to write in this workbook. Use the worksheets. Make the book your own. Record advice from your mentor, the results of actions that you take, and your assessment scores. Make this book tell *your* mentoring story. It then becomes your record and your "personalized" reference tool.

This book is divided into six sections:

The Power of Mentoring

Strategy #1: Seek Greater Self-Awareness

Strategy #2: Crystallize Your Vision

Strategy #3: Concentrate on a Manageable Number of Potentially High-Growth or Advancement-Opportunity Outcomes

Strategy #4: Excel at Maximizing Your Time with Your Mentor

Strategy #5: Stay Focused on Your Goals or Outcomes

Introduction

A successful mentoring experience can put more pizzazz into your career advancement and professional development and provide you with important benefits, such as professional exposure, expert advice, and access to prime resources. But it takes work. This is a quick-read application book that helps you get the most out of your mentoring experience, whether you currently have a mentor or are searching for one, and whether you are engaged in an informal mentoring experience or one that is more formal.

In many respects, you share the driver's seat with your mentor; you cannot be passive. In fact, getting the most out of your mentoring relationship is a multistep process. However, it is practical and straightforward: As the protégé, you need to be serious and deliberate in your quest for success. In this book, we will explain how to take expert aim, using five strategies for protégé success. The worksheets, models, and tools included will help you implement the strategies.

The Five Strategies

The five strategies for protégé success are:

1. Seek greater self-awareness.

2. Crystallize what it is you hope to achieve from the mentoring relationship relative to your career vision or goals for professional-advancement.

3. Concentrate on a manageable number of potential outcomes with high growth or advancement (connection to experts or power-brokers, leadership skill building, etc.).

4. Maximize your time with your mentor. Apply what you learn and tap into his or her resources (people, organizations, knowledge, etc.).

5. Stay focused on your goals.

The Power of Mentoring

Before getting to the details of the five strategies, let us discuss the power of mentoring and examine several kinds of mentoring. Talent is unquestionably critical to the lifeblood of any organization; that is why effective processes designed to attract, develop, and retain leadership talent are worth every penny. A well-conceived and executed mentoring program is an investment that can pay dividends: keen decision makers, adept project managers, and great team builders make money for their organizations!

Mentoring is a popular subject in management literature. A *mentor* is generally considered to be a senior-level leader who takes an active interest in promoting the career of a more junior individual. Significantly, mentoring is an important factor in a protégé's career, related to salary, promotions, and career satisfaction. In addition, these kinds of outcomes can act as performance motivators for the protégé.

However, don't think of mentoring as simply a traditional one-on-one relationship between a more experienced leader (mentor) and a less-experienced individual; mentoring can take a variety of forms.

3

Mentoring Formats

Informal Mentoring

Informal mentoring can be described as guidance, support, and discussion that is casual and often social. Specific goals are not usually defined, and the mentoring tends to be spontaneous or on an "as needed" basis. The mentor and the protégé may have met by chance and not because of an organized effort to seek mentoring. The informal mentoring relationship tends to evolve naturally, so it won't be consistent in terms of the number, length, and planned outcomes of mentor-protégé contacts.

However, this does not mean that you cannot and should not formalize some goals for the experience. The goals can be informal—they do not have to be etched in stone, but can instead be fluid, while still providing some focus for the experience. Just be sure you have some vision of where you want your career to go.

Formal Mentoring

Formal mentoring can be described as a structured method used for coaching, development, and advancement. It can also help achieve specific organizational goals, such as developing leadership skills and succession planning. Contacts or sessions between the mentor and the protégé are scheduled or planned relative to frequency, length, format, and even content. The content could be divided into several categories, such as the following:

- Sharing (sharing experiences, points of view, resources)
- Advising or recommending
- Reviewing (reviewing work, progress on development actions, outcome of contact with experts)
- Relationship building or socializing
- Network building (connecting with individuals with influence, expertise, or position power)

The content of the mentoring sessions provides intrinsic rewards in the form of achievement, information acquisition, and personal relationship. It also provides a development planning framework. This book contains a number of useful tools that support development planning.

One-on-One Mentoring

One-on-one mentoring is perhaps the most familiar form of mentoring, particularly in the organizational setting. Individualized attention helps the protégé establish goals and objectives, and solve problems; the mentor is focused exclusively on that one individual for that period of time. Generally, a close bond forms that builds trust and confidence.

Group Mentoring

In group mentoring, a protégé derives support, ideas, professional alliances, and even friendships with other protégés in the group. It can be stimulating to be surrounded by others who are working toward similar goals and enhancing their own lives. A potential downside of group mentoring is that less-outspoken or withdrawn people may be neglected.

(Note: If you are introverted and are in a group-mentoring situation, you might want to work on a development goal aimed at helping you be more able at participating actively in a group. You might also use additional ways of communicating with your mentor [such as e-mail] and try to maximize your time with your mentor [Strategy #4]. Take advantage of networking opportunities with other protégés, and try to identify a positive role model from whom you can learn.)

Cross-Cultural Mentoring

Cross-cultural mentoring is all about creating mentoring relationships with people from different cultural or ethnic backgrounds. This enriches cultural understanding within the context of career movement or professional development, and raises one's appreciation for diversity by creating an open dialogue between participants in the program. Organizations sometimes use this form of mentoring as part of diversity and inclusion initiatives. Cross-cultural mentoring can be done one-on-one or in groups.

Benefits of a Mentoring Experience

Mentoring brings several benefits, as you can see from the list below. Can you think of more?

Mentoring can . . .

- Expand your network.

- Expand your knowledge in a targeted area.

- Help you improve your project management skills.

- Add to your resources (relevant books, articles, workshops, white papers, etc.).

- Give you exposure to key figures in your organization or professional circle.

- Provide quality feedback regarding development opportunities.

- Help you develop your skill in a targeted area.

Strategy #1

Seek Greater Self-Awareness

Mentoring is a form of teaching or instructing through consultation. From the protégé's point of view, it is a kind of learning through consultation: As a protégé, you work in tandem with your mentor in a learning/development partnership. "Partnership" is the key word: To be successful, both parties must be engaged at full throttle. In some respects, the gain or benefit from the partnership is reciprocal, but typically, it is the protégé who is on the "learning" side of the equation. However, that side of the equation is an exciting place to be! This is especially true if as the protégé you are *purposeful* in your actions, seizing every learning opportunity the experience offers in order to gain personal insight. The information in this book, as well as the surveys, worksheets, tips, and models, will help you as you take that journey.

As we said at the outset, success takes work. Be very deliberate in your aim for a successful mentoring relationship.

Look for a good fit.

It is important that you understand what you need in a mentor. It has to be a good fit—not just a good fit between you and your mentor, but also between you and the whole mentoring process. Mentoring is not just "social time." If the relationship seems to be moving in that direction more and more, reconsider the relationship and what you want to achieve. This individual might be a better friend than a mentor. If this becomes the case, look for another individual who is able to be more effective in the role.

What makes a good protégé?

A protégé is an individual whose career is furthered by a person of experience, prominence, or influence. Is there such a thing as a good protégé? We'll look at this subject in this section of the book.

Certain attitudes and abilities can increase your success as a protégé. For fun, think of your potential for being a good protégé as falling into one of four categories: full throttle, first gear, second gear, and third gear. "Full throttle" is the most desirable category; it is reflective of such actions and qualities as effective communication, motivation, openness to change, career visioning, and receptivity to feedback. You'll find several tools in this section that will help you assess your potential for getting more out of a mentoring relationship. Try using some or all of them.

Checklist of Protégé Qualities

Quality	Does the statement describe me?	
	Yes	No
1. I am comfortable sharing my personal assessment of my development needs.		
2. I am comfortable sharing my work challenges.		
3. I look at and receive feedback in the spirit of gaining insight into potential development opportunities.		
4. I know how to translate developmental feedback into specific actions for improvement/change.		
5. I am open to making changes and growing, knowing that it will be difficult, but will pay off in the long run.		
6. I am willing to make the time for the mentoring relationship.		
7. I know how to use informal feedback or coaching to my advantage.		
8. I am willing to be flexible during the mentoring relationship. It may not be exactly what I envisioned, but I'm willing to see if "different" turns out to be better.		

What is your capacity for maximizing the mentoring experience?

An essential ingredient in mentoring and other developmental processes is self-awareness. That is the purpose of the self-assessment that follows. It will help you identify your *current ability* and *potential* for maximizing every opportunity the mentoring experience presents. And after all, you have to know where you are before you can create an improvement plan and move forward.

Read each statement on the self-assessment survey and rate yourself from 1 to 4 (1 = To a Little Extent; 2 = To a Moderate Extent; 3 = To a Great Extent; and 4 = To a Very Great Extent). There are 34 statements. As you read each statement, ask yourself how effective you are at whatever action is described.

Note: If you are not currently in a mentoring relationship, rate the statements according to how you feel you would behave or the degree to which you would achieve the action described in the question.

The self-assessment will help you gain an appreciation for the types of actions that support maximizing the mentoring experience and perhaps encourage you to talk them over with your mentor. If you take it at the inception of the relationship and at regular intervals to measure improvement (such as every quarter), you will enhance the experience.

Instructions for Completing the Self-Assessment Survey

This is what the survey looks like. It contains 34 statements related to protégé skills and behaviors.

Maximize Every Opportunity: Self-Assessment Survey

1 = To a Little Extent 3 = To a Great Extent 2 = To a Moderate Extent 4 = To a Very Great Extent	1	2	3	4	Points
1. I have a clea___ mentoring r___			x		3
2. Although I h___ out of the m___ enough to m___				x	4
3. Although I h___ out of the mentoring relationship, I am comfortable ___expected outcomes.		x			2
___my mentoring relationship. ___dvice into action and let ___e.				x	3

Place a checkmark or an x in the appropriate box, based on how you assess yourself on the question. Rating Scale: 1–4

Place the point value (1–4) for your response to the statement in this column.

			Total Points		

Add up your numbers in the "Points" column to determine your total score. The total score can range from 34 to 136.

Score Range
Full Throttle: **110–136**
Third Gear: **90–109**
Second Gear: **65–89**
First Gear: **34–64**

Avoid Pitfalls

Be honest in taking the survey and in discussions with your mentor. This is essential to maximizing your relationship. Do not feel like you have to be perfect. Being a successful protégé is a process, like most things in life.

Maximize Every Opportunity: Self-Assessment Survey

1 = To a Little Extent 3 = To a Great Extent 2 = To a Moderate Extent 4 = To a Very Great Extent	1	2	3	4	Points
1. I have a clear vision of what I want to get out of a mentoring relationship.					
2. Although I have a clear vision of what I want to get out of the mentoring relationship, I am still flexible enough to modify my vision.					
3. Although I have a clear vision of what I want to get out of the mentoring relationship, I am comfortable with unanticipated or unexpected outcomes.					
4. I am an active partner in my mentoring relationship. I translate my mentor's advice into action and let him/her know the outcome.					
5. I have developed my career vision or professional advancement goals.					
6. I have created or thought through a life plan for myself.					
7. I have created or thought through a hierarchy of my development needs relative to meeting my career/professional vision.					
8. I prepare for sessions or exchanges with my mentor by identifying one primary need (information, advice, a listening ear, etc.) for each session/exchange.					
9. I discuss the work projects or problems that have the greatest growth value with my mentor.					
10. After a session/exchange with my mentor, I systematically review or revisit the experience and document information or insights I gained.					
11. I put the information or insights gained from my mentoring experience into action.					
12. I seek developmental feedback from my mentor.					
13. I talk over challenging tasks or work-related interpersonal experiences with my mentor so that I can get his/her perspective or advice.					

(continued)

Maximize Every Opportunity: Self-Assessment Survey *(continued)*

1 = To a Little Extent 3 = To a Great Extent 2 = To a Moderate Extent 4 = To a Very Great Extent	1	2	3	4	Points
14. I am sensitive to my mentor's time schedule and availability.					
15. I use a variety of ways (such as e-mail, voice mail, and social activities) to stay in contact with my mentor, unless my mentor has one preferred way he/she would like to be contacted.					
16. I am comfortable initiating contact with my mentor.					
17. I ask my mentor what he/she expects of me (if anything) regarding matters such as when or how often to meet.					
18. I ask my mentor what he/she expects of me (if anything) regarding preparation for meetings (e.g., read an article, bring a report to review, prepare an answer to a question).					
19. I am comfortable with impromptu meetings or sessions with my mentor.					
20. I can handle impromptu assignments/requests from my mentor effectively.					
21. I proactively address developmental roadblocks with support from my mentor.					
22. I revisit my developmental goals with my mentor periodically to identify any needs for adjustments.					
23. I make adjustments to my developmental goals as the need arises.					
24. I seek ways to thank my mentor for his/her professional generosity (e.g., thank-you note, thank-you e-mail, verbal thanks, sharing information of value to my mentor, such as an article or a book).					
25. I am open to making changes or seeking continuous improvement.					

(continued)

Maximize Every Opportunity: Self-Assessment Survey *(concluded)*

1 = To a Little Extent 3 = To a Great Extent 2 = To a Moderate Extent 4 = To a Very Great Extent	1	2	3	4	Points
26. I am comfortable asking my mentor for referrals to help expand my network.					
27. I periodically ask my mentor for recommendations on relevant books, articles, workshops, white papers, Web sites, audiotapes, and so on.					
28. I use active-listening skills during meetings or exchanges with my mentor (e.g., I use positive and open body language, reflect back what I hear, mentally focus on key points, and make consistent eye contact).					
29. I use effective verbal communication (discussion) skills during meetings or exchanges with my mentor (e.g., I express my ideas with clarity, use concrete examples that relate directly to my points, and ask open-ended questions to elicit more-specific input from my mentor).					
30. I use effective persuasion skills when presenting or defending my position on an issue with my mentor.					
31. I am comfortable meeting in an office setting (mentor's office, boardroom, meeting room, etc.).					
32. I am comfortable meeting in a social setting (lunch, golf tournament, professional association conference, etc.).					
33. I can comfortably handle interruptions to a meeting/session with my mentor.					
34. I reward myself for accomplishments that result directly or indirectly from my mentoring relationship.					
			Total Points		

What's your score?

Are you going at full throttle?

First Gear (34–64)	Second Gear (65–89)
You have room to improve your ability to maximize the benefits of mentor feedback and guidance, and leverage developmental opportunities.	You are gaining momentum, but there is still room to pick up speed to reach full throttle.
Third Gear (90–109)	**Full Throttle (110–136)**
You have good momentum. You are almost there in terms of capitalizing on the advantages of the mentoring experience.	You are going at full throttle by maximizing the benefits of your mentor's feedback, knowledge, experience, and guidance (social, political, etc.). You know how to leverage the benefits of the mentoring experience into professional development actions.

Motivation Drivers

What motivates you relative to work performance? Motivation is a major factor in why people choose to engage in particular behaviors in particular ways. People vary greatly in the drivers that motivate their behavior. Identifying your motivators can help you refine your career plan and make better use of your mentor's support.

Self-motivation is an essential ingredient in effective mentoring. The chart below contains some general categories of motivation "drivers." Where do you fit? What is your primary driver? The chart divides motivators into four general categories.

Work Performance Motivators

Motivators	Characteristics
Achievement	• Loves the act of achieving something • Enjoys sharpening job skills to reach greater heights • Is generally pleased to receive a "stretch" assignment (that is, an assignment that requires knowledge or skill growth)
Influence	• Thrives on having influence and control such as being an in-house expert • Welcomes the attention and the feeling of importance that comes with having some authority (e.g., being in charge of a project team or a high-visibility assignment) • Seeks center stage at meetings or gatherings
Affiliation	• Wants to feel a sense of ownership • Likes to build relationships with team members • Finds the social aspect of a job very satisfying • Enjoys getting to know team members in informal settings, such as a softball team outing, offsite retreat, or staff picnic
Value	• Is sensitive to how ideas/suggestions are perceived • Can respond in a negative way if perceived as being disregarded or dismissed • Appreciates recognition and feedback • May have a high need for recognition, acknowledgment, and other things that maintain or reinforce esteem • Likes to support and recognize others

Think about your primary motivation driver when you are trying to understand which assignments or suggestions from your mentor you will likely have more affinity toward. What does a job or assignment require? What is important to you in your relationship with your team? How does that affect your interactions with them? Perhaps you will be in a better position to explain why you did not reach your goal or need improvement on a work assignment or interpersonal situation if you understand yourself better. When you try to translate your mentor's advice, etc., into usable actions, be sure you know what motivates you the most.

Determining/Prioritizing Your Motivators: Worksheet

Directions: Which of the development options below do you find most appealing or motivating? Why? Place a checkmark in the boxes or rank them in order of priority importance from 1 to 13 (with 1 being the highest).

☐ New technology or access to new technology (software or hardware)

☐ A high visibility or "plum" assignment

☐ Group work or involvement (member of implementation team, etc.)

☐ Job rotation

☐ Job shadowing

☐ Special project

☐ Participation or lead on a key committee

☐ Role-playing sessions

☐ Leadership fast-track program

☐ Project lead

☐ Public recognition

☐ Attendance at seminar or workshop

☐ Executive MBA

Change/Adaptability

Changing or responding to new opportunities can be an exciting outgrowth of a mentoring relationship. How do you feel about change? How receptive and comfortable would you be to making a behavioral change or taking on a "growth" project suggested by your mentor?

Of course, there's no simple formula to determine how you will respond to a particular change. It might depend on factors such as the nature of the change, the timing, or the circumstances. However, you probably do have a general tendency in terms of how you initially react to changes in your personal or work life.

The worksheet on the next page is a fun way to look at how you generally respond to change. Which of the four metaphors best describes you? Why? Reflect on your feelings about change, and make a few notes in the space provided. Start by responding to the metaphor at the left that you most closely identify with. Then comment on the ones you disagree with.

Response to Change: Worksheet

	This best describes (or does not describe) my attitude toward personal change because . . .	This best describes (or does not describe) my attitude toward professional or work-related change because . . .
Change is like a roller-coaster ride. It is both exhilarating and frightening.		
Change is like a new pair of shoes. It is tight and uncomfortable until you break it in.		
Change is like a hailstorm. It is fast and furious, and you just have to ride it out.		
Change is like a hot fudge sundae. It is delicious and satisfying, and leaves you eagerly anticipating the next one.		

Compare styles.

One way of seeking greater self-awareness is to compare your style with your mentor's style relative to behaviors that are essential to an effective relationship. Try using the survey below to jump-start a conversation with your mentor about communication-style compatibility.

You and your mentor should each complete the survey. Try to compare your results during your first or second meeting: You can compare your responses and discuss what and how much you have in common, or discuss the possible impact of having many things in common (or few) on the success of your relationship. If you are already involved in a mentoring relationship, you could still use the survey as a talking point regarding, for example, communication styles or preferences.

The majority of the questions focus on communication and collaboration. There are no right or wrong answers. The goal of the survey is to provide a context for conversation about compatibility for a mentoring relationship.

Comparing Styles: Survey

Directions: Read each statement and determine if it describes you *most* of the time. Check off "yes" or "no" in the appropriate column.	Yes	No
1. I like to share information, ideas, and opinions.		
2. I like/prefer to think about an issue first, formulate my opinion, and then share my response.		
3. I tend to form an opinion quickly on an issue, and enjoy voicing my opinion almost immediately.		
4. I like/prefer to use stories or metaphors to explain concepts or situations.		

(continued)

Comparing Styles: Survey *(concluded)*

Directions: Read each statement and determine if it describes you *most* of the time. Check off "yes" or "no" in the appropriate column.	Yes	No
5. I like/prefer that concepts or situations are explained in a plain, straightforward way.		
6. I like being challenged to independently figure out a solution to a problem or situation.		
7. I like collaboration or back-and-forth dialogue for figuring out a solution to a problem or situation.		
8. I appreciate the importance of looking at a situation from different views when seeking a solution to a problem.		
9. I like to rely on my past experience with a situation when seeking a solution to a problem.		
10. I like/prefer face-to-face exchanges, as opposed to voice-to-voice or communication by e-mail.		
11. I like/prefer to have frequent contact with a mentor (or protégé).		
12. I am comfortable with "virtual" meetings or exchanges (primary contact by e-mail or messaging).		
13. I like/prefer working from an agenda for formal meetings with a mentor (or protégé).		
14. I am aware that there are some gender-related differences in communication styles.		
15. I am aware that there can be culture-related differences in communication styles.		
16. I like the Socratic method of asking a protégé open-ended, challenging, or quiz-type questions to prompt or expand thinking.		
17. I like/prefer preparing and presenting questions to a mentor for his/her response (advice, recommendations, etc.) as a development technique.		
18. I prefer not to be concerned with the structure of interactions (e.g., meetings) with a mentor, but to instead go with the flow.		

Strategy #2

Crystallize Your Vision

Vision: The Beacon for Your Mentoring Experience

Like the beacon in a lighthouse that guides a vessel through familiar but sometimes unpredictable seas, you need a clear vision to guide your mentoring experience. Before you search for a mentor or participate in a mentoring experience, pay attention to this essential step.

Draw yourself a mental picture of what you hope to ultimately achieve by participating in a mentoring relationship. Now take that activity a step further: Write down what that picture means in terms of a specific overarching goal. (For example, your overarching goal might be to expand your "power" network by gaining access to people with influence or sought-after expertise.) Now put this goal in writing to crystallize it and revisit your goal as circumstances warrant.

Is Your Career Vision 20/20? A Questionnaire

Ask yourself these critical questions:

- What is my short-term career goal? (What goal do you want to implement within the next six months to a year?)

- What is my immediate career goal?

- Where do I see myself, in terms of my career, ten years from now?

- Do my short-term and immediate goals support my long-term career goals?

- What talents do I have that will support my career goals?

- What abilities do I need in order to reach my career goals?

- Is there any additional development (professional exposure, targeted work experience, education) I need in order to meet my career goals?

- In my ideal career situation, how do I want to work? What kind of time commitments would best suit me? What degree of creative avenues would I like? What degree of autonomy would I like?

My career vision is . . .

Career Vision Statement

A career vision statement can be useful in crystallizing where you want to go with your career. It should include these components:
  • The ideal job/career
  • Work and personal values that support the job/career
  • An overall strategy for achieving the job/career

Additionally, you plan and direct your career through three levels of action, which become the components of the Career Self-Management Model: *self, opportunity,* and *strategy*. All three levels of action work together to produce a dynamic career-development process that results in:
  • Knowing your interests, talents, skills, and values.
  • Understanding the requirements (education, experience, etc.) for various career or job opportunities.
  • Creating a sound strategy for career or job movement.

Career Self-Management Model

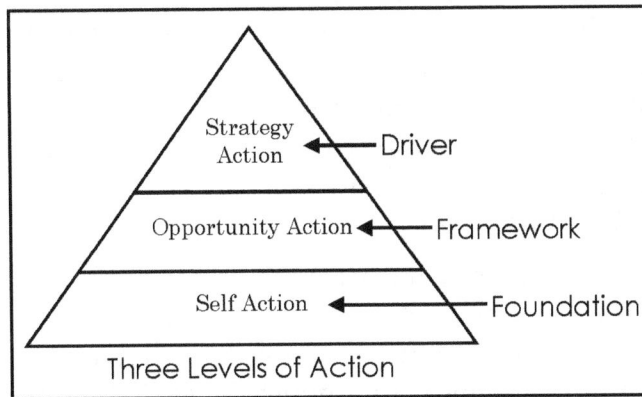

Strategy Action — Driver

Opportunity Action — Framework

Self Action — Foundation

Three Levels of Action

Self-Management

Introspection (or looking inward) is essential to career self-management. It produces strategic awareness of your skills, interests, intrinsic job rewards (i.e., factors that make you feel recognized and satisfied), the fit of your personal values with a job or career, and the fit of your performance capabilities with a job or career. Additionally, it provides a framework for maximizing your personal and professional effectiveness.

Opportunity

Awareness of and appreciation for opportunities at different levels can be essential to personal career management. The concept of different levels refers to upward and lateral opportunities. The fact that potential development and growth (e.g., skill building, knowledge building, behavioral change) exist at two levels is a core aspect of opportunity vision.

Strategy

You must translate into a realistic career strategy the insight you gain from understanding your skills, interests, and values and having greater knowledge about job/career opportunities. Career movement occurs through planning and strategizing. Most important, it is fueled by your initiative and support from your mentor or your organization. You are the driver. Self-advocacy (in terms of committing to a career vision, setting clear and achievable goals, and developing steps to reach the goals) is a primary outgrowth of strategy vision, which includes the following styles:

- Develop a portfolio of your accomplishments.
- Identify skill-growth opportunities.
- Prepare for job selection processes (i.e., behavioral-based interviews, panel interviews, role plays, in-baskets, simulations, etc.) through planning and practice.

The next two pages contain tools you can use to crystallize and track your career vision.

26

Career Vision: Worksheet

Name: _____	Date: _____

Where do I visualize myself in the next three years, in terms of my personal life and career life?

What specific goals will support achieving my vision?

Goal	Investment (what's needed to implement; how will I implement)	Yield (results/benefits relative to my five-year vision)	When (date for implementation)
#1			
#2			
#3			

Revisiting my plan:

Date	Summary of Revisit	Modifications needed as result of revisit

My career action statement is . . .

My resources are . . .

Professional Advancement: Tracking Tool

Name: _____ **Date:** _____

What professional advancement goal do I visualize for myself?

☐ Short-term goal
☐ Long-term goal

What skills, experience, and education or training do I need in order to achieve my career goal?

Skills	Experience	Education or Training

What specific goals and actions will help me achieve my vision?

Goal: What do I need to do to achieve my vision (broader experience/ expertise, training certification)	Action: How will I meet my goals (training, degree, special assignment, project lead opportunity)	When: When will I take action? (date or time frame)	Completion check-off
1.			
2.			
3.			
4.			
5.			
6.			
7.			

Development Planning

Being systematic about your job or career development planning involves looking at where you are (perhaps with your mentor) and identifying what is required for a particular job. Organize yourself by concentrating on target job characteristics, such as these:

- Experience
- Education
- Interpersonal style that best suits the job (team player, self-directed, etc.)
- Knowledge
- Job structure (e.g., 50 percent travel, 17 direct reports, high visibility)

For each of these characteristics, identify the gap—the difference between *Where I am now* and *What's required for the job.*

The tools on the next several pages are designed to help you close the gap by strategizing with your mentor which actions will best prepare you for the job.

Job/Career Requirements Targeting Tool
(What's essential for the job?)

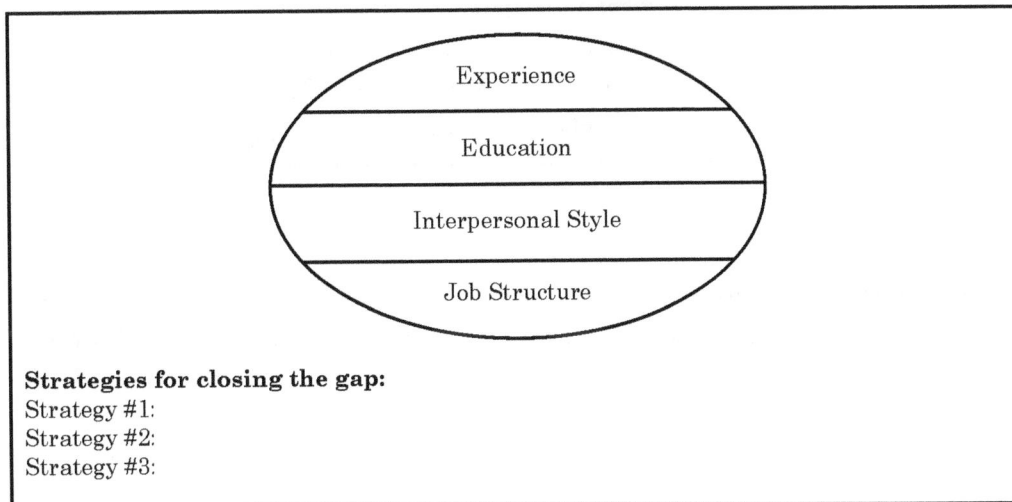

Experience

Education

Interpersonal Style

Job Structure

Strategies for closing the gap:
Strategy #1:
Strategy #2:
Strategy #3:

Consider your career plan. Look at your development planning in terms of how closely it matches or fits in with your career plan. Discuss any accomplishments or roadblocks with your mentor. Seek ideas from your mentor on assignments, projects, and resources that can help you achieve your goal. Use the definitions below to help you with this step:

- **Accomplishments**—the real situation or task, the action taken, and the end result

- **Relationship to career goal**—contribution to reducing the gap between current job or career and target job or career

- **Significance**—the impact on your individual performance goals, department initiatives (if appropriate), personal satisfaction, personal insight, etc.

Career Planning Tool

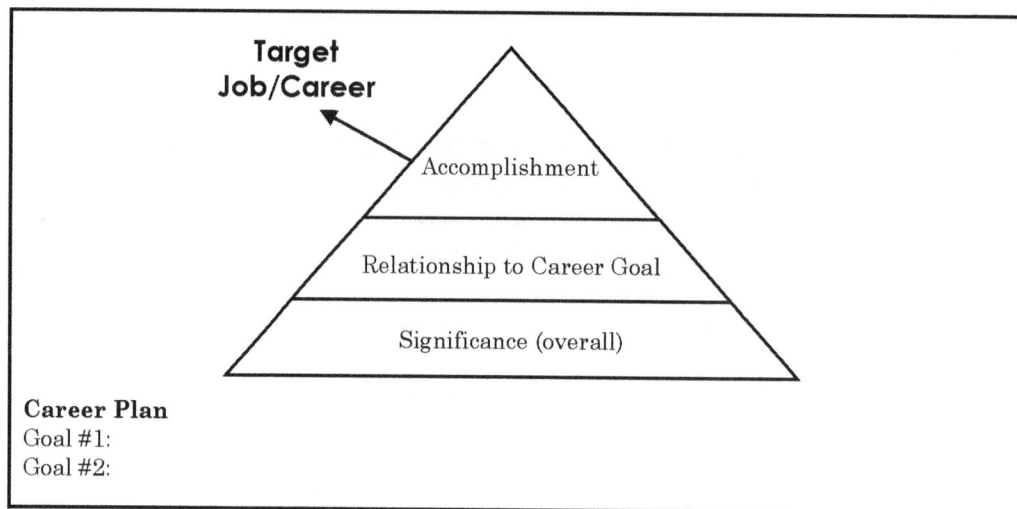

Target Job/Career

Accomplishment

Relationship to Career Goal

Significance (overall)

Career Plan
Goal #1:
Goal #2:

The tools on the next few pages are also useful in development planning.

Self-Development: Worksheet

Name: _____	Date: _____

My overall development goal is . . .

The actions or sources I will pursue are the following:

Source (books, articles, self-assessment tools or processes, journaling, peer feedback, client feedback, mentor feedback)	Action Date

The primary insight I gained about myself regarding talent, interests, values, and skills is this:

Talents	Interests	Values	Skills

My strategy for using the newly gained or reinforced awareness is . . .

Closing the Gap: Worksheet

	My current level	The requirements for the job or career	My plans for closing the gap (e.g., seeking ideas from my mentor regarding training education, certification; gathering information from books, articles, Web sites; using assessment instruments; seeking special assignments that would be beneficial)
Education			
Experience			
Skills			
Interpersonal style			
Knowledge			

Job Analysis: Worksheet (Part 1)

Job structure (requirements) What is essential for the job? (extended hours, building networks, travel, point person on major projects, politicking)	Preferred structure (What is my work style/preference? What are my personal values relative to work and family?)	Gap (What are the key differences? And do I want to modify my preferences?)	
Planning for closing the gap		**Date Started**	**Date Completed**
Strategy #1:			
Strategy #2:			
Strategy #3:			

Job Analysis: Worksheet (Part 2)

	Next Steps (How will I use what was gained?)
What did I achieve or gain by implementing Strategy #1? (knowledge, skill, awareness, perspective, etc.)	
What did I achieve or gain by implementing Strategy #2? (knowledge, skill, awareness, perspective, etc.)	
What did I achieve or gain by implementing Strategy #3? (knowledge, skill, awareness, perspective, etc.)	

Job Skills and Experience: Inventory

Directions: Review the job description and talk to other people who have held the job. Then complete the chart below.

Main duties/responsibilities of the job (e.g., track legislation, identify grant-funding opportunities, supervise sales staff)	Primary job outputs or results (e.g., implementing marketing campaigns, developing proposals)	Interpersonal qualities desired for the job (e.g., team player, self-directed, extroverted)

Tracking Tool for Completing Goals

Date: _____		
Accomplishment (situation/task, action taken, end result)	**Relationship to career goal** (contribution to reducing gap between current job and target job)	**Significance** (overall impact on my individual performance goals, department initiatives, personal satisfaction, personal insight, etc.)

Strategy #3

Concentrate on a Manageable Number of Potentially High-Growth or Advancement-Opportunity Outcomes

What growth outcomes would you like to realize from the mentoring relationship? Growth outcomes can refer to personal development, professional development, skill enhancement, or career outcomes. It is essential that you think about what you expect from the sessions or exchanges you have with your mentor and prioritize them. This is easier to do if you have a formal mentoring relationship, where meetings are set up or arranged and program outcomes are sometimes preordained. Of course, mentoring does not always fit into a neat box; your mentoring relationship, for example, might not have an overall focus. Whatever form your mentoring takes, think through what you'd like it to be like, and ask your mentor to share his or her expectations. Several worksheets to help you organize your desired outcomes are included in this section.

We have been focusing on career or job advancement, but there are other outcome categories. Identify your needs or interests relative to tangible (and sometimes intangible) outcomes of the mentoring experience by first reviewing the categories that start on the next page.

Outcomes and Goals

It is possible that you and your mentor will decide on an area to focus on right away, but the focus area might simply evolve during the course of the first few meetings. The following information should help you define your mentoring goals.

Project Management or Implementation Tactics

Perhaps your greatest need or interest is to improve your management or implementation of projects, including the "people" side of project management. What aspects of project management are you struggling with? Try seeking feedback from peers or clients regarding your project-management skills to help you pinpoint your development needs. Also, try self-reflection to further pinpoint your development needs. A worksheet that can be used for capturing and assessing lessons learned is included in the next section (page 52).

Inclusion or "Glass-Ceiling" Issues

Cross-cultural or cross-gender mentoring generally involves some discussion about so-called glass-ceiling issues. Discrimination is a delicate and controversial subject, but if you truly want help addressing this kind of problem, it is essential that you discuss the subject candidly with your mentor. Determine whether or not your mentor is the best person to help you address problems related to inclusion, and be sure you are open to divergent points of view.

Career or Job Movement Strategies

Career or job movement is often a focus of mentoring. This subject was discussed in the previous section of this book.

Networking

Your primary need might be to benefit from your mentor's influence in the organization. Perhaps you are seeking opportunities to establish connections with individuals who can provide you with information or support for a project, or help advance you in your career. It could be that you simply want to expand your own influence through affiliation. Whatever your goal is, you need to clearly articulate it to yourself and to your mentor. The more your goals are in focus, the better.

Targeted Leadership Skill Building

Perhaps you are interested in improving a specific leadership skill (strategic thinking, budget management, building constituencies, etc.). Engage in a discussion with your mentor regarding why you want to focus on a particular skill. Is lack of competency in a certain area holding you back from advancement? Are you having difficulty with a particular skill that is essential to success in your current job? Is there an organizational initiative regarding leadership? Work with your mentor to identify ways to help you develop the skills you need. Your mentor might be able to provide you with solid suggestions.

Behavioral-based Feedback

A mentor can be a great source of performance feedback. If your mentor is someone who has the opportunity to observe or debrief your performance (live action, a report you prepared, a decision you made, etc.), arrange for him or her to make relevant comments regarding the following: the actions taken or behavior, the degree of effectiveness or ineffectiveness of the actions, recommendations for alternative actions if the ones taken were ineffective, and the potential benefits of the alternative actions.

Social Interaction

Your need might simply be to make social contact with an individual in a senior-level position who can guide you when a situation requires it. Perhaps you are interested in relationship building for future support or sponsorship on projects or career advancement. You do not have to have developmental goals in mind—even social contact is a goal.

What other reasons for mentoring can you identify?

Setting Goals at the Start of the Mentoring Relationship

It often helps to put your needs and goals in writing at the beginning of the mentoring relationship. Taking the time to identify the areas you want to focus on will keep you and your mentor on the same track throughout the mentoring experience. The goals or outcomes might not be immediately clear and they might even need to be changed or modified later on. A written roadmap can also serve as a record of what you have been doing.

A sample mentoring worksheet appears on the next page.

Engagement Worksheet

Mentor:_____ Date: _____

Protégé: _____

Focus of the session or exchange	Specifics of the problem, situation, or need	Desired outcome/change	Actions (based on input from mentor)
Project management or implementation tactics			
Inclusion or "glass ceiling" issues			
Career/job movement strategies			
Networking (connection to experts, knowledge-brokers, etc.)			
Targeted leadership skill building (strategic thinking, setting broad policy, building constituencies, etc.)			
Behavioral-based feedback (actions taken, degree of effectiveness, recommendations for alternative actions, benefits of alternative actions)			

The sessions can also focus on the kinds of interaction you will have with your mentor, such as these:

- Discussion

- Sharing experience, knowledge, ideas, or information

- Advising or recommending (e.g., activity, resource, expert, action, etc.)

- Listening

- Reviewing (e.g., work progress on development actions, outcome of contact with expert, etc.)

Looking at the process from this view provides another way to create focus for your sessions.

Use the tool on the next page to help you organize your thoughts before you meet with your mentor. The idea is to think about a specific development goal and the type of exchange that will help you close the gap. (For example, you might want to use your mentor's knowledge and experience to create an effective way to develop and present a business case for new hardware.)

Session/Exchange Worksheet

Overall Goal: _____

Kind of exchange with mentor (and relevant details)	Description of support that would help me meet my goal (development, career, performance)	Date scheduled
Discussion		
Sharing experience		
Recommending activity		
Connecting with resource or expert		
Listening		
Reviewing work		
Recommending resources		

Strategy #4

Excel at Maximizing Your Time with Your Mentor

You and your mentor undoubtedly have work responsibilities and personal lives. The time you will be able to carve out together will be limited, so make the most of it.

Focus and preparation are essential if you want to maximize your time with your mentor. Monitoring your progress is another key step.

Prioritize your development goals.

Prioritizing your development goals can help you use your mentoring time judiciously. Identify the top *development, growth, or career-advancement goals* on which you want to focus initially. Use your list as a framework for seeking *specific* support from your mentor. Here are a few ways to do this:

- Brainstorm a list of needs, and then arrange them chronologically, by importance, or by widest potential impact.

- Write down your needs in a notebook or journal as they arise. You could then prioritize your list once a month or prior to meetings with your mentor.

- Target work projects or issues for discussion with your mentor that have the greatest growth value for you.

Prepare for meetings.

If you have scheduled meetings with your mentor, set aside some time to prepare. Your preparation might simply be to identify what you want to talk about, or to bring information about an assignment you would like to talk over with your mentor.

Here is one format for formal mentoring meetings:

Part 1: Dialogue
You and your mentor should engage in detailed conversation about the focus of the meeting (review of performance report, advice/guidance on new project, expansion of knowledge, coaching on acquiring new or modifying existing behaviors, building a relationship, etc.). Dialogue provides the opportunity to work on the relationship and build trust.

Part 2: Feedback
The next part of the meeting can consist of feedback: positive and developmental information, tips, recommendations, and examples that help you proceed. This is the time to review previous development or action plans.

Part 3: Action
Before the meeting is over, create an application plan or series of steps for applying new skills, knowledge, or information. You can also designate tactics for addressing challenges, and lay out steps for introductions and networking with experts.

Even if your exchanges with your mentor are not formal meetings, you can still think in terms of the dialogue, feedback, and action format. The goal is to have some sort of framework for your exchanges with your mentor.

Of course, you do not have to prepare for meetings in a formal way. Jotting down a few notes might work for your situation (especially if you are not involved in a formal mentoring relationship). The point is to prepare so that you can maximize your time with your mentor.

Anticipate roadblocks.

Try to anticipate roadblocks (problems, inhibitors to success, etc.). At a minimum, keep your antennae up and scan for possible roadblocks that prevent you from:

- Finding enough time or the right time to spend with your mentor.
- Implementing suggestions from your mentor.
- Preparing (in a broad or specific way) for meetings with your mentor.
- Completing assignments requested by your mentor (looking up information, reading an article, contacting someone, etc.).

Think through in advance how you will respond to a roadblock.

Put the information or insights you gained into action.

Debrief challenging tasks or interpersonal experiences with your mentor and get his or her perspective and advice. Capture the information in some way (take notes, use a checklist, etc.). This section includes a "debrief" worksheet to use after a mentoring session (page 49).

Track your progress.

Track your progress in using what you gain or learn from the mentoring relationship. Systematically review/revisit each mentoring exchange or session and document information or insights you gained. Journaling and tracking tools are good ways to gauge your progress. Several tracking tools are included in this and the next section; modify them or create your own.

Session Worksheet

Mentor:_____ Date: _____

Protégé: _____

Focus of the session or exchange	Specifics of the issue, situation, or need	Desired outcome/ change	Actions (based on input from mentor)	Date of Completion
Project management or implementation tactics				
Inclusion or "glass ceiling" issues				
Career/job movement strategies				
Networking (connection to experts, knowledge-brokers, etc.)				
Targeted leadership skill building (strategic thinking, setting broad policy, building constituencies, etc.)				
Behavioral-based feedback (actions taken, degree of effectiveness, recommendations for benefits of alternative actions)				
Social interaction				

Debrief of Mentoring Session

Date: _____ Overall Goal:_____

Scope of the session or exchange	Value (how it can be used)	Application opportunity (where it can be used—project, situation, customer, etc.)	Change/ improvement
Discussion			
Sharing experience			
Recommending activity			
Connecting with resource or expert			
Listening			
Reviewing work			
Recommending resources			

Goal Tracking: Worksheet

	Date: _____
Goal Category	**Notable Milestone Resulting from Goal** Describe, in action terms, the following, as appropriate: customer response, leader recognition, successful completion of major project, acquisition of new business, completion of training or education, successful development or use of new skill, additions to network. Include, where applicable, quantity, quality date, and/or output.
Knowledge increase/new learning	
Skill/competency enhancement (interpersonal, technical)	
Education advancement	
Networking/ relationship building	
Project/idea implementation (work, personal)	

Personal and Professional Accomplishments Tool

Date: _____	
Directions: Summarize your personal accomplishments during the last six months that grew out of input from your mentor (suggestion, connection to resources, constructive feedback, etc.). Use additional paper, if necessary.	
1.	
2.	
3.	
4.	
5.	

Reflections/Lessons Learned

Looking back at a situation from a lessons-learned perspective is a great way to improve your skills. This kind of debrief allows you to anticipate what you might do differently in the same or a similar situation. Through the lessons-learned process, you can pinpoint needs for development or support.

Questions for Reflection

Ask yourself these questions following a project or problem-solving experience:

- Were the right tactics or actions employed?

- How well did the tactics that were employed work?

- What factors, if any, impacted the degree of success of the tactics?

- What new ideas, if any, can be gleaned from the situation? How can you use these new ideas?

- Were any potential root causes of the situation revealed? (It could be helpful to use a root-cause analysis methodology to uncover the underlining causes of the problem.) If so, what were they?

- Was the problem or the circumstance that precipitated the problem similar to any past situations? If so, how?

- What key learning will you implement from the lessons-learned activity? (change in behavior or method; new way of looking at something; inclusion of additional or different data in decision making, etc.)

- What resources will you need?

- When is the best time to implement? Should you implement gradually or in phases?

- Will you need to involve others?

- What is the overall benefit of the implementation?

Discuss these questions with your mentor and seek input from him or her.

Strategy #5

Stay Focused on Your Goals or Outcomes

Periodically examine where you are.

We already discussed the importance of tracking your progress, but you must also look at where you are in relation to your goals, formally or informally. If you are involved in a formal program sponsored by your organization, it is likely that your organization has an evaluation process to help you accomplish this. A few ideas that can be used to track your progress are described below:

- Keep an electronic or a paper-based journal of your progress. Review all the entries periodically.

- Set up a schedule for meetings or exchanges with your mentor (biweekly, bimonthly, or quarterly) to discuss your goals and the steps you're taking toward those goals.

- Use an assessment tool to evaluate your progress.

- Keep a calendar listing of goal-related activities or actions (contact with an expert suggested by your mentor, implementation of a new idea discussed with your mentor, practice of revised behavior recommended by your mentor, etc.).

- Maintain a list of achievements.

Self-scoring assessment instruments that look at a number of key components related to effective mentoring are included in this section of the book.

Stay focused.

Two "stay focused" surveys are included in this section. The surveys are designed to help a protégé periodically evaluate (e.g., once a quarter, at the end of a year-long formal mentoring process) the effectiveness of the mentoring relationship. The stay-focused assessment tools can be used by an individual or an organization for evaluating how well the program is going.

Stay Focused: Periodic Assessment #1 (pages 56–57) examines four areas related to mentoring: feedback, interaction, action planning, and overall value. The assessment asks a series of questions related to each area, for a total of 16 questions. You are asked to choose one of four responses for each question to help you assess the degree to which you are meeting your goals. The closer you are to the total possible points (64), the better your mentoring relationship is progressing relative to the elements the tool examines. Discuss using such a tool with your mentor.

Stay Focused: Periodic Assessment #2 (page 58) examines seven elements for evaluating progress. You are asked to determine your degree of satisfaction and/or benefit regarding each element that applies to you. The objective is to assess the following elements numerically and anecdotally:

1. Regularly scheduled meetings

2. The partnership with the mentor (the mentor's availability, receptivity to the process, etc.)

3. Development planning activities

4. Development feedback/advice

5. Access to the mentor beyond scheduled time

6. Development programs offered by your organization

7. External workshops or products for development

Goal Assessment Strategy

The goal assessment tool that closes this section is one way of laying out a six-month timeline for your mentoring experience. The goals do not have to be major ones—they can be the intermediate steps needed to accomplish a major outcome. The objective is to identify the steps and determine a strategy for assessing them.

Stay Focused: Periodic Assessment #1

Date: _____

0 = Does not apply 1 = To a Small Extent 3 = To a Great Extent 2 = To a Moderate Extent 4 = To a Very Great Extent	0	1	2	3	4	Points
Feedback from mentor (advice, information sharing, results of review of work, opinion, etc.) **Interactions with mentor** (meeting, phone conversation, conversation at an event, impromptu meeting, etc.)						
Is the feedback targeted to the outcomes that have been agreed upon by you and your mentor?						
Is the feedback readily useful and applicable?						
Is the feedback developmental in nature?						
Do you discuss with your mentor how to apply any feedback that you receive from him/her?						
Has the feedback and/or the interactions contributed to behavioral change (e.g., more-consistent use of interpersonal style that elicits team support)?						
Has the feedback and/or the interactions contributed to skill improvement (e.g., better management of complex projects)?						
Has the feedback and/or the interactions contributed to knowledge gain (e.g., understanding the impact of federal legislation on marketing a product)?						
Action planning with mentor						
Have development outcomes been identified and agreed to by you and your mentor?						
Have development actions been identified that will help achieve the outcomes?						
Has scheduling/holding structured sessions contributed to successful implementation of the actions?						

(continued)

Stay Focused: Periodic Assessment #1 *(concluded)*

0 = Does not apply 1 = To a Small Extent 3 = To a Great Extent 2 = To a Moderate Extent 4 = To a Very Great Extent	0	1	2	3	4	Points
Action planning with mentor *(continued)*						
Has progress on implementation of the actions been tracked?						
Have roadblocks to success been discussed?						
Have alternative actions been discussed or implemented to address roadblocks?						
Overall value						
Are you satisfied, overall, with your protégé-mentor match?						
Overall, is the mentoring experience helping you directly or indirectly in achieving your career vision?						
Overall, is the mentoring experience providing the benefits you expected?						
Total Points						

57

Stay Focused: Periodic Assessment #2

Date: _____		

Directions: Using a scale of 1–4 (4 being the highest), assess your degree of satisfaction and the benefits of the mentoring experience up to this point, based on each of the seven process elements listed in the column on the left. Include notes or comments.

Mentoring Process Elements	Rating	Notes or Comments
Regularly scheduled one-on-one meetings with the mentor		
The "partnership" with the mentor: the mentor's availability, receptivity to the process, genuine interest in your development, etc.		
Development planning activities (identifying development actions, tracking progress, addressing roadblocks, etc.)		
Developmental feedback/advice from the mentor		
Access to the mentor over and above scheduled one-on-one meetings		
Development courses, programs, and products offered in your organization		
External workshops, programs, and products recommended by your organization		

Goal Assessment Strategy Tool

Timeline	Description of mentoring goal	Strategy for assessing achievement of goal	Goal met?	
			Yes	No
Month 1				
Month 2				
Month 3				
Month 4				
Month 5				
Month 6				

59